EXCITING TITLES FROM

Scobre EDUCATIONAL

"Because practice makes perfect."

Contemporary Fiction & Sports Adventures

TALES OF THE UNCOOL
6-Book Series

These are the stories of the nerds, geeks, and freaks of Halsey Middle School — and how six self-proclaimed 'uncool' tweens took over their school.

Grades: 4-6
Ages: 8-12
Pages: 64

Paperbacks: $8.99
Library Bound: $27.99

MAGIC LOCKER ADVENTURES
6-Book Series

Three young friends find a magic locker, which takes them back In tIme. Historic sporting events are in jeopardy unless they right history!

Grades: 3-5
Ages: 8-11
Pages: 48

Paperbacks: $8.99
Library Bound: $27.99

ON THE HARDWOOD 30-Book Series

MVP Books invites readers to stand alongside their favorite NBA superstars *On the Hardwood*. These officially licensed NBA team bios provide an exciting opportunity to learn about where a team has been, and where they are going...

Grades: 4-6
Ages: 8-12
Pages: 48

Paperbacks: $8.99
Library Bound: $27.99

Common Core Aligned

 twitter.com/bookbuddymedia   facebook.com/bookbuddymedia

ORDER NOW!

Contact Lerner Publisher Services:
www.LernerBooks.com
Call: 800-328-4929 • **Fax:** 800-332-1132

Lerner
PUBLISHER SERVICES

WORLD CUP

BY JUSTIN PETERSEN

World's Greatest Sporting Events: World Cup

Copyright © 2015
Published by Scobre Educational
Written by Justin Petersen

Printed in the United States of America.

Scobre Educational
2255 Calle Clara
La Jolla, CA 92037

Scobre Operations & Administration
42982 Osgood Road
Fremont, CA 94539

www.scobre.com
info@scobre.com

Scobre Educational publications may be purchased for educational, business, or sales promotional use.

Cover and layout design by Jana Ramsay
Edited by Zach Wyner
Copyedited by Renae Reed
Some photos by Newscom

ISBN: 978-1-62920-152-8 (Soft Cover)
ISBN: 978-1-62920-151-1 (Library Bound)
ISBN: 978-1-62920-150-4 (eBook)

INDEX

INTRODUCTION

Every four years, hundreds of thousands of dedicated soccer fans pour into a host city, decorated in the vibrant national colors of their country, prepared to cheer their lungs out and celebrate the beautiful game. The World Cup features some of the world's greatest athletes, playing the world's most popular sport. It is a tribute to those that have devoted their passion, skill, energy and imagination to the fulfillment of one goal— bringing a World Cup to their country.

Started as an alternative to the Olympic Games soccer tournament, the World Cup has grown in size to rival the Olympics as the world's largest sporting event. In 2010, more than one-seventh of the world's population tuned in to watch the final between the Netherlands and Spain. It's easy to understand why this event is so popular. World Cup drama is a product of what takes place on the **pitch** as well as international politics, and it has not been without controversy. The 1938 Italian champion infamously saluted

Spain celebrates their first-ever World Cup title in Johannesburg, South Africa.

its quarterfinal opponent, France, with the fascist Nazi salute. In 2010 and 2014, many argued that the money invested in new stadiums in South Africa and Brazil should have gone to building hospitals and schools in poor communities.

Despite its problems, no one can deny the World Cup's incredible power. Soccer fans travel thousands of miles and spend vast amounts of money to witness history, while players dream and sacrifice throughout their lives for the opportunity to represent their country. Those few players that achieve their dreams and earn a World Cup championship become living legends.

Fans travel great distances, at considerable expense, to cheer on their country's national team.

A Look Back

Soccer, known outside of the United States as "football," was formally invented in 1863 in England and shortly thereafter, a number of clubs united to form the **London Football Association**. Despite the fact that its primary audience was members of the upper class, the sport's popularity rapidly grew, spreading like wildfire to every corner of the globe.

Soccer's explosion owed much to its simplicity. While some sports require a lot of equipment, anybody with a ball and access to a field can play soccer. Makeshift **goalposts** can be made out of cones, trash cans, backpacks or old pairs of shoes. If there aren't enough people around for a full game, players circle up and practice ball control, using their feet, thighs, chests and heads.

In 1872, the first international soccer match featured teams from England and Scotland. By the early 1900s, it was clear that international soccer tournaments were ready to expand beyond the United Kingdom. Soccer was featured

Soccer's popularity grew because of its beauty and simplicity.

Uruguay's national team poses at the 2014 World Cup.

at the Olympic Games in 1900 and 1904–the same year in which the Fédération Internationale de Football Association (FIFA) was founded in Paris, France. In its first year, seven countries participated in FIFA. Within a year, this number swelled to 15. Using the annual game between England and Scotland as a model, FIFA decided to hold an annual tournament.

After some early stumbles, the first World Cup was played in Uruguay in 1930. It had humble beginnings, with only 13 teams playing for the world title, and it was no surprise when the powerful Uruguayan team defeated Argentina in the final. While 80,000 fans were on hand for the match, it was mostly a home crowd due to the high price of travel.

Brazil's world famous Meracana Stadium, site of the 1950 and 2014 World Cup Final.

As compared to today, far fewer fans had the means to go all the way to South America for a sporting event. However, just like the sport of soccer, the tournament proved to be an unstoppable force that grew in power and influence with each year.

In 1950, with the United States still recovering from World War II, the U.S. World Cup team upset powerhouse England. The victory inspired millions of Americans and ignited a newfound appreciation for the sport. That same year saw Uruguay win their second World Cup, defeating Brazil in the front of nearly 200,000 spectators at Brazil's famous Meracana Stadium. While the defeat stung, it would be the last time that Brazil would lose a World Cup final for quite some time. In 1958, a 17-year-old Brazilian star by the name of Pelé exploded onto the international stage. Pelé scored six goals in four World Cup games, including two in Brazil's 5-2 win over Sweden in the final. By the time all was said and done, Pelé would lead Brazil to three World Cup titles. He was the captain and Golden Ball award winner with the 1970 Brazilian champion, a team that to this day is considered by many to be the finest **national team** ever assembled.

Pelé celebrates after scoring a goal in the 1970 World Cup.

Since its inception, the World Cup has evolved to include qualification rounds and a higher number of participating nations in the final phase. In 1984, the field grew from 16 participants to 24, and at the 1998 World Cup in France, that number again increased to its current size of 32 teams. In order to include more Asian and African nations, a plan to expand the number of participants to 40 nations is in the works.

One would think that the more countries there are competing for the title, the less likely a country would be to win multiple

Famed striker Cristiano Ronaldo led Brazil to their fifth World Cup championship in 2002.

championships. However, over the years there have been a few countries that have consistently made the finals and won the cup, despite the rise in competing nations. Brazil is the all-time leader in World Cup titles with five, while Germany and Italy have both won four. In 2014, Germany became the first European team ever to win a World Cup title on South American soil, when they defeated Argentina, 1-0, in Brazil's Maracana Stadium.

Germany celebrates their country's World Cup victory in 2014.

TIMELINE

1942 AND 1946
Because of World War II, the World Cup is twice postponed. Some believed this signaled the end of the tournament, but football had gained too much popularity for the World Cup to be snuffed out by war.

1900 **1925** **1950** **1975**

1904
FIFA is founded in Paris, France. Their early efforts to create an international soccer tournament are unsuccessful.

1938
Italy wins its second straight title, becoming the World Cup's first repeat champion.

1958
Led by soccer sensation Pelé, Brazil wins their first World Cup title.

1930
French footballer Lucien Laurent scores the first goal in the history of the World Cup.

1966
England, the country in which soccer was born, wins their first World Cup. Geoff Hurst becomes the first player to register a **hat trick** in a World Cup final. The British team defeats West Germany, 4-2.

1970
Led by Carlos Alberto and Pelé, Brazil goes 6-0 in tournament play and becomes the first nation to win three World Cup titles. This Brazilian team is considered one of the best in World Cup history.

2010
South Africa becomes the first African nation to host the tournament. Spain defeats Netherlands, 1-0, to win their first World Cup title.

1986
Argentinean hero Diego Maradona scores two of the most famous goals in World Cup history—"The Hand of God" and "Goal of the Century"—leading Argentina to a 2-1 quarterfinal victory over England. Argentina goes on to beat West Germany, 3-2, and capture their second World Cup title in three tournaments.

1980	1990	2000	2010

1982
The World Cup expands from 16 to 24 teams.

1998
The format of the World Cup again changes, allowing 32 teams to play in the final stage. France unexpectedly crushes huge favorite Brazil, 3-0. Emmanuel Petit scores the last World Cup goal of the millennium.

THE FUTURE

Thanks to the Internet, and a global community of fans, soccer has taken root in the United States. While the sport was already hugely popular in South America, Africa, Europe and the Middle East, it has seen a surge of interest in Asia as well. With the 2014 World Cup TV ratings topping those of the World Series, it's clear that this tournament has a bright future. As FIFA looks to expand the final stage to 40 teams, more countries in Asia and Africa anticipate becoming participants in this beloved event.

EQUIPMENT

One of the reasons that soccer enjoys such worldwide popularity is that the only equipment required to play is a ball. However, the equipment used at the highest levels of play has advanced a great deal over the past century.

The ball: Originally, the soccer ball was made of leather. However, this presented problems in certain climates, as it would become heavy when wet. The modern ball was invented in 1951. It was made with 32 panels of plastic-coated fabric; 20 of which have six sides and 12 of which have five sides. In addition to the new materials, another major advancement was that it had no laces. In order to be inflated, a hook-like needle can be inserted through one of its panels. The new material also made it much easier to keep the ball at its proper weight of 14 to 16 ounces.

The shirts/jersey/kits: With the development of new fabrics, the jersey has and continues to evolve. Originally, jerseys were made of thick cotton, but toward the end of the 1960s, lighter and cheaper materials were used. Today's players have the advantage of playing in extremely light jerseys that do not absorb moisture.

Defenders need the most protection and wear a heavy shin guard with ankle protection. Forwards need a lighter shin guard that allows for greater mobility.

Footwear: Soccer **boots** (known in the United States as "cleats") have changed dramatically since the beginning of the 20th century. They first were made out of sturdy and durable leather. Nowadays, synthetic materials allow the boot to be thinner and lighter, allowing players to maneuver with greater speed and agility.

Protection: **Shin guards** are the only protection worn by players. They are mandatory and extremely important.

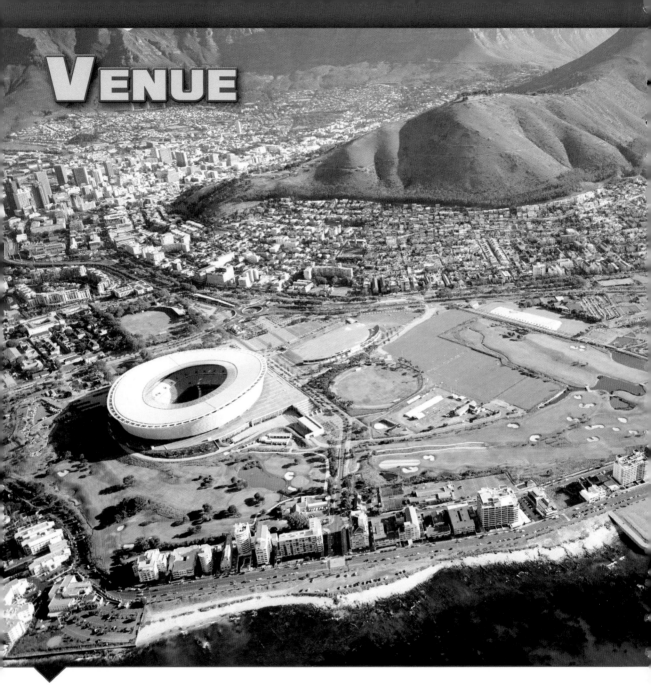

VENUE

An aerial view of the Cape Town soccer stadium,
built for the 2010 World Cup in South Africa.

The host country is decided years before the event to allow all the time necessary for a country to improve and/or construct new venues. Traditionally, FIFA tries to alternate between different regions of the globe. The World Cup first came to the United States in 1994, and in 2002, Korea and Japan co-hosted the tournament, marking the Cup's first appearance in Asia. In 2010, South Africa became the first African country to welcome the event.

In order to be selected, a country must submit a plan that includes an estimated cost for the upgrade and/or building of stadiums. After the tournament has ended, the stadiums

A view of the sunset over Moscow, Russia. Russia will host the World Cup in 2018.

are generally still used by local teams or are modified to welcome concerts or other sports. Only two stadiums–Mexico City's Azteca Stadium and Brazil's Maracana Stadium– have hosted multiple World Cup finals.

In developing countries, World Cup stadiums often go unused once the games are done. In South Africa, FIFA demanded 10 new stadiums, but because of the high cost of maintenance and the poverty across the areas in which they were built, many of these stadiums now stand empty. While hosting the World Cup may bring fame to the host nation, it can also bring financial hardship and frustration to its people.

Rules

Soccer is a game played between two teams. It consists of 11 players, including one goalkeeper. The winning team is determined by whoever scores more goals. The game is 90 minutes long, and is divided into two halves of 45 minutes with a 15-minute break for **intermission**.

The pitch is of rectangular shape, and should be between 100 and 130 yards long and 50 to 100 yards wide. However, in international football, the regulations are stricter, with the pitch measuring between 70 and 80 yards wide and 110 to 120 yards long. Advances in goalpost design have seen them change from rectangular prisms to cylinders. This way a ball has a chance of bouncing off the post and into the goal. The goal is eight yards wide and three yards high. In order for a goal to be allowed, the ball has to cross the line entirely. With the development of GoalControl-4D technology, shots can now be reviewed, making it possible to reverse mistakes by the referees.

Coaches use chalkboards to illustrate their team's strategy.

Referees congratulate each other at the conclusion of the 2014 World Cup Final.

The referee and his two assistants, also called linesmen, are in charge of enforcing the rules on the pitch. The fourth official is in charge of checking the boots of substitute players as they come off the bench and announce any added time. If a referee gets injured, the fourth official serves as a replacement. The linesmen indicate if a player is offside, which team benefits from a **throw-in** and call fouls. Players can earn a yellow card for rough play. After a second incident, players are given a red card and ejected from the game.

THE ROAD TO...

The qualification phase starts two years before the World Cup. Every member nation competes to send their team to the final phase. The groups are made within the same geographic region, which means a team from North America cannot face a South American team. Different numbers of slots are allocated to different regions of the World. These slots reflect the number of the nations in a given region. Given the history of strong European teams, and the high number of countries in a relatively small region, Europe is awarded the most slots with 13.

Every country wants to defend its colors, but ultimately the 32 best get this chance. As it currently stands, this number includes 5 African teams, 13 European, 4.5 South American, 3.5 North and Central American and Caribbean (**CONCACAF**), 4.5 Asian and 0.5 from Oceania. The reason for the ".5" figure is that some of these teams have to compete against teams from other continents to qualify. For example, South America's last team to qualify needs to have a playoff game against another CONCACAF team to earn the final spot.

In 2014, Costa Rica was a pleasant surprise, finishing first in their group and advancing to the quarterfinals.

Spain was unable to take advantage of their top seed in the 2014 World Cup, failing to make it out of the group stage.

The final phase consists of a group stage, the round of 16, the quarterfinals, the semifinals and the final. There are eight groups of four teams. Securing the top spot in a group often proves crucial in a championship run.

Best Performances

EUSEBIO DA SILVA FERREIRA, 1996

Eusébio "The Black Panther" da Silva Ferreira was born on the east coast of Africa in Mozambique. Because Mozambique was a colony of Portugal, Eusébio played for the Portuguese national team.

In 1966, Portugal faced a surprising North Korean team in the quarterfinal round. North Korea started strong, scoring three goals in the first 31 minutes of the game to take a 3-0 lead. Then Eusébio took over. The Portuguese star scored two goals before halftime and then two more in the first 15 minutes of the second half. His four straight goals led Portugal to a 5-3 victory and cemented his legacy as one of the greatest big-game scorers of all time.

ZINEDINE ZIDANE, 1998

Named the best European football player of the past 50 years by Union of European Football Associations (UEFA), Zinedine Zidane earned France's Legion of Honor medal for his play in the 1998 World Cup.

One of the best players in the history of the game, Zidane remained humble and elegant throughout his career. He was a true superstar, playing his best when the lights shone brightest. In the 1998 World Cup Final, he scored twice, propelling France to their first World Cup championship—a 3-0 victory over defending-champion Brazil. Zidane went on to have an incredible career at Juventus and Real Madrid, both world-class European soccer clubs.

RONALDO LUIS NAZARIO DE LIMA, 2006

Ronaldo Luís Nazário de Lima, Brazil's second-best goal scorer behind the legendary Pelé, is one of only three men to win the World Player of the Year award three times.

Battling injuries and a growing chorus of voices that claimed he was not the player he had once been, Ronaldo showed the world that he was far from finished. With two goals against Japan, he became just the 20th player in World Cup history to score in three World Cup tournaments. His goal against Ghana in the Round of 16 gave him 15 career World Cup goals, breaking the all-time scoring record set by German footballer Gerd Muller.

JUST FONTAINE, 1958

Born in Marrakech, Morocco, Just Fontaine played for the French national team in the 1958 World Cup and set a record that may never be broken.

In 1958, Just Fontaine scored 13 goals in the final stage of the World Cup in Sweden. Unfortunately for Fontaine, his remarkable efforts were not enough to propel the French to the Word Cup final, as they fell to the mighty Brazilian team in the semifinal match. His team's defeat did not diminish his amazing achievement. Fontaine's 13 career World Cup goals are still third best in the history of the tournament, despite the fact that he only played in one tournament.

THE RECORD BOOK

With five World Cup championships, Brazil leads all nations in international football excellence.

In 1958, Just Fontaine scored 13 goals, leading France to the tournament semifinals

Mario Zagallo and Franz Beckenbauer are the only two footballers to have won the World Cup both as players and as coaches. Zagallo is the only man to win it twice as a player and once as a coach.

No team has experienced more heartbreak than the Netherlands. They have advanced to three World Cup finals but lost each time.

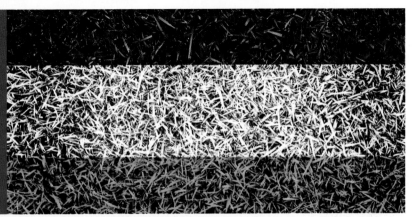

Hungary scored 27 goals in 1954, setting a record that stands 60 years later. They fell in the final to West Germany, 3-2.

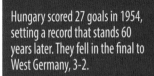

In 2014 German **striker** Miroslav Klose broke Brazilian legend Ronaldo's World Cup scoring record with his 16th career World Cup goal.

THE FANS

The World Cup gained millions of new fans in the United States in 2014.

Soccer fans sacrifice just about anything for their team. In some regions of the world, people joke that fans work hard just so they can afford to go support their favorite teams in person on the weekend. And that's just at the club level. Imagine then the feelings that motivate fans of this sport to cheer on their countrymen in the World Cup—a collection of the greatest soccer players from all over the world, playing in a tournament that only comes around once every four years. Millions of fans make travel plans years in advance of a World Cup. Meanwhile, the World Cup final attracts a larger television audience than any other sporting event in the world.

German soccer fans celebrate their team's fourth World Cup championship in 2014.

1954 was a crucial year for World Cup soccer, as, for the first time, the games were televised. This forever changed the sport and increased the popularity of the tournament. With the development of the Internet, viewers and spectators experience the games in an even deeper way, as they feed on a steady diet of analysis and **statistics**, as well as updates from the players themselves.

One billion people watched the 2010 World Cup on TV, roughly one-seventh of the entire world's population. With soccer's popularity reaching new heights in the U.S., viewership numbers were even higher. The World Cup final was the most watched soccer game in U.S. history as an estimated 26.5 million people tuned it.

IMPACT

It goes without saying that the World Cup has a significant place in the hearts of people who love soccer. Included amongst these are the players who train and sacrifice for months and even years, with the hope of one day representing their country as well as their home fans. However, what sets the World Cup apart from almost all other sporting events is the impact that it has on people who don't follow the sport.

The World Cup's footprint is massive. In order to host a World Cup, countries need to renovate or build new stadiums and sometimes relocate entire communities. The cost in dollars is in the billions. But the toll the World Cup takes on the host country cannot be measured in money alone. Still, with all its challenges, the World Cup provides countries with an opportunity to demonstrate to the world what they can do when they pull together. As long as soccer remains the world's most popular sport, nations will line up to host soccer's most popular tournament.

Construction is underway on the Kazan Arena stadium in Kazan, Russia, host of the 2018 World Cup.

GLOSSARY

boots: boots (called cleats or soccer shoes in North America) are an item of footwear worn when playing association football.

CONCACAF: The Confederation of North, Central American and Caribbean Association Football, commonly known as CONCACAF, is the continental governing body for association football in North America, Central America and the Caribbean.

goalposts: two vertical posts, called the goal posts, supporting a horizontal crossbar.

hat trick: the scoring of three goals in a game by one player.

intermission: also known as "halftime," the intermission is the pause or break in the action that occurs at the 45-minute mark in a soccer match.

London Football Association: the regional Football Association for Greater London. The London FA was established in 1882 and is affiliated with the Football Association.

national team: a team that represents a nation, rather than a particular club or region, in a sport.

pitch: the playing surface for the game of football made of turf.

shin guard: a pad worn to protect the shins when playing soccer.

statistics: numerical data that measures the effectiveness of players.

striker: an attacking player, especially one who positions themselves near the opponent's goal in the hope of scoring.

throw-in: the act of throwing the ball from the sideline to restart play after the ball has gone out of bounds.